EXTREME WEATHER

DROUGHTS

NorwoodHouse Press

JACK WILLIAMS

Cataloging-in-Publication Data

Names: Williams, Jack.
Title: Droughts / Jack WIlliams.
Description: Buffalo, NY : Norwood House Press, 2026. | Series: Extreme weather | Includes glossary and index.
Identifiers: ISBN 9781978576957 (pbk.) | ISBN 9781978576964 (library bound) | ISBN 9781978576971 (ebook)
Subjects: LCSH: Droughts--Juvenile literature.
Classification: LCC QC929.25 W555 2026 | DDC 363.34929--dc23

Published in 2026 by
Norwood House Press
2544 Clinton Street
Buffalo, NY 14224

Designer: Rhea Magaro
Editor: Kim Thompson

Photo credits: Cover, p1. Skripnik Olga, Nick Starichenko /Shutterstock.com; p. 5 justkgoomm/Shutterstock.com; p. 7 Piaffe Photography/Shutterstock.com; p. 8 Leonid Ikan/Shutterstock.com; p. 9 Lizard/Shutterstock.com; p. 10 Bilanol/Shutterstock.com; p. 11 jokerpro/Shutterstock.com; p. 12 mariakray/Shutterstock.com; p. 13 PBouman/Shutterstock.com; p. 15 vitec/Shutterstock.com; p. 16 pio3/Shutterstock.com; p. 19 Rokas Tenys/Shutterstock.com; p. 20 Edgar G Biehle /Shutterstock.com

Printed in the United States of America

TABLE OF CONTENTS

WATCH OUT!

The ground is dry.

Rivers are low.

Plants **wilt**.

Watch out! It is a **drought**.

WHAT IS A DROUGHT?

In a drought, the weather is unusually dry. Not much rain falls.

Droughts can last weeks, months, or years.

Usually, a **rainforest** gets lots of rain. A grassland gets a medium amount of rain.

Sometimes, a rainforest or grassland gets much less rain than usual. Then, it is in a drought.

Water and air flow around Earth. Their patterns control the rain in different **climates**.

These patterns can change. Then, droughts can happen.

Droughts happen slowly. It takes a long time for **soil** to dry out.

Droughts go away slowly. It takes a long time for enough rain to fall.

WHY ARE DROUGHTS DANGEROUS?

Droughts harm plants. Plants need water to grow. Dry soil can blow away. Farm **crops** can fail.

In dry forests, **wildfires** can start.

Droughts harm people and animals.

There may not be enough water to drink. There may not be enough food.

HOW TO STAY SAFE

Watch the weather **forecast**. It will tell you if there is drought in your area.

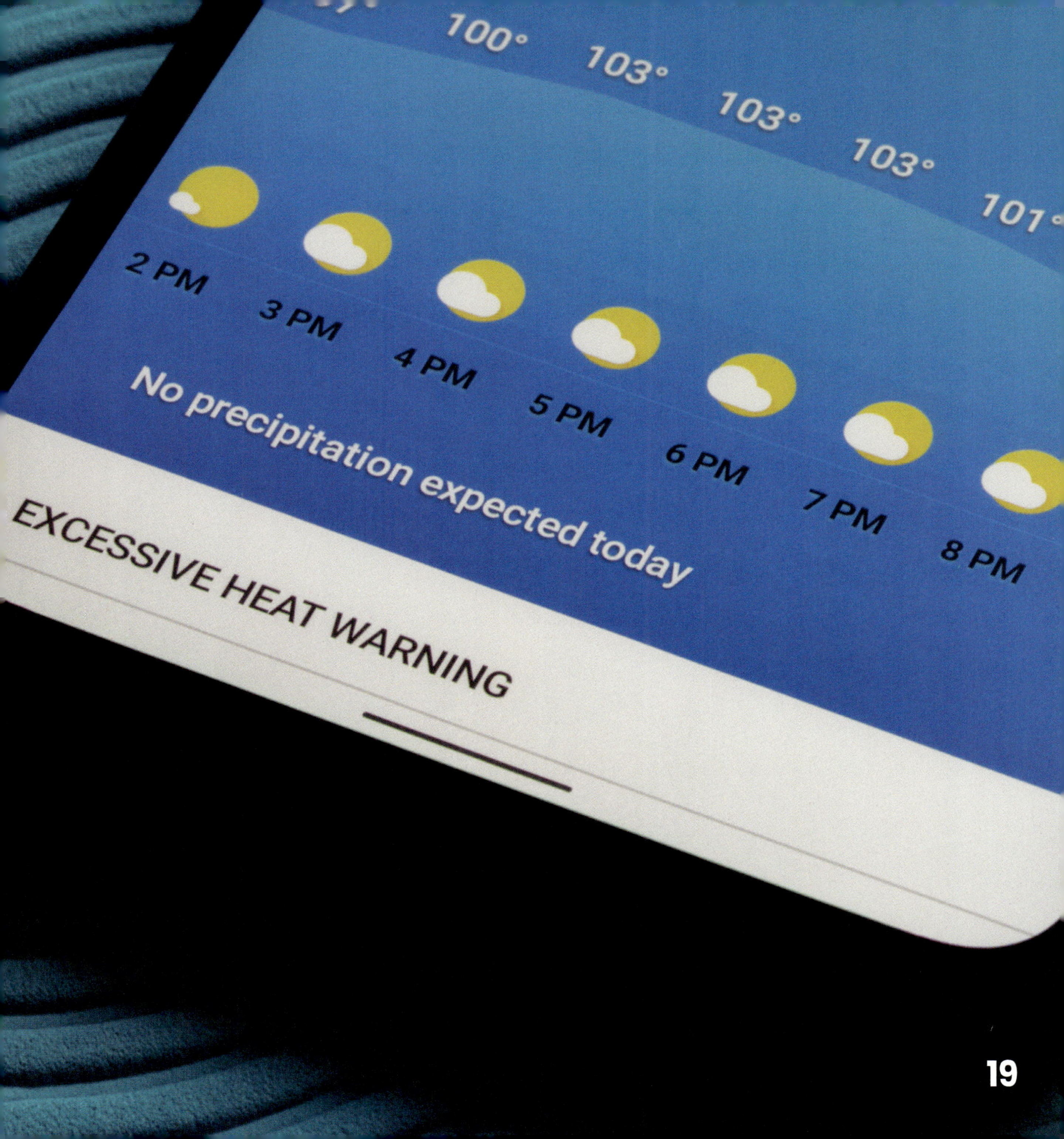
100°
103°
103°
103°
2 PM
3 PM
4 PM
5 PM
6 PM
7 PM
8 PM
No precipitation expected today
EXCESSIVE HEAT WARNING

Farmers can use special **methods** that protect the soil.

People can **conserve** water. They should not waste any water.

GLOSSARY

climates (KLYE-mits): the usual weather in places over a long period of time

conserve (kuhn-SURV): to save or use less of something so it does not run out

crops (krahps): plants grown as food for people and animals

drought (drout): a long period without enough rain

forecast (FOR-kast): a report that tells what the weather will be like in the future

methods (METH-uhds): ways of doing things

rainforest (RAYN-for-ist): a dense, tropical forest where a lot of rain falls

soil (soil): the dirt that covers Earth's surface and provides a home for plants

wildfires (WILDE-fires): uncontrolled fires that burn natural areas

wilt (wilt): to bend and droop due to lack of water

THINKING QUESTIONS

1. How long can droughts last?
2. How long can it take droughts to go away?
3. How do droughts harm plants?
4. How do droughts harm people and animals?
5. What does it mean to conserve water?

INDEX

ABOUT THE AUTHOR

Jack Williams is curious about all things in nature, especially the weather! He checks the weather forecast every day. He used to be a police officer, so he knows how important it is to watch out for danger and stay safe.